# Praise for Nancy Naomi Carlson's
# *Stone Lyre:*

"René Char is the conscience of modern French poetry and also its calm of mind. Carlson, in these splendid translations, casts new light upon the sublime consequence of Char's poetic character."

—DONALD REVELL

"Early Surrealist, resistance fighter, anti-nuclear activist, and throughout it all, exquisite poet, René Char is at the heart of twentieth-century French poetry. . . . Carlson gives English-language readers a real sense of Char's depth and breadth. And her masterful translations catch the barely contained drama that gives Char's work such tension and presence, while her excellent ear picks up not only the sound relationships that weave through the originals, but also their delicate, seductive rhythms."

—COLE SWENSEN

"René Char, intrepid explorer of the marvelous, witness to the catastrophe of history, plowman of 'the metered field,' stands revealed in Nancy Naomi Carlson's splendid translations as a guiding spirit of our time."

—CHRISTOPHER MERRILL

### Tupelo Press Poetry in Translation

*Abiding Places: Korea, South and North*, by Ko Un
Translated from Korean by Hillel Schwartz and Sunny Jung

*Invitation to a Secret Feast: Selected Poems*, by Joumana Haddad
Translated from Arabic by Khaled Mattawa with Najib Awad, Issa Boullata,
Marilyn Hacker, Joumana Haddad, Henry Matthews, and David Harsent

*Night, Fish and Charlie Parker*, by Phan Nhien Hao
Translated from Vietnamese by Linh Dinh

*Stone Lyre: Poems of René Char*
Translated from French by Nancy Naomi Carlson

*This Lamentable City: Poems of Polina Barskova*
Edited by Ilya Kaminsky and translated from Russian by the editor
with Katie Farris, Rachel Galvin, and Matthew Zapruder

*New Cathay: Contemporary Chinese Poetry*
Edited by Ming Di and translated from Chinese by the editor with Neil Aitken,
Katie Farris, Christopher Lupke, Tony Barnstone, Nick Admussen, Jonathan
Stalling, Afaa M. Weaver, Eleanor Goodman, Ao Wang, Dian Li, Kerry Shawn
Keys, Jennifer Kronovet, Elizabeth Reitzell, and Cody Reese

*Ex-Voto*, by Adélia Prado
Translated from Brazilian Portuguese by Ellen Doré Watson

*Gossip and Metaphysics: Russian Modernist Poems and Prose*
Edited by Katie Farris, Ilya Kaminsky, and Valzhyna Mort,
with translations by the editors and others

*Calazaza's Delicious Dereliction*, by Suzanne Dracius
Translated from French by Nancy Naomi Carlson

*Canto General: Song of the Americas*, by Pablo Neruda
Translated from Spanish by Mariela Griffor

René Char

*Le Marteau sans maître*

*Translated by*
*Nancy Naomi Carlson*

Tupelo Press
*North Adams, Massachusetts*

*Hammer with No Master.*
*Le Marteau sans maître*

Copyright © 1934 and 1945 Librairie José Corti, Paris.
Translation copyright © 2016 Nancy Naomi Carlson. All rights reserved.

Library of Congress Cataloging-in-Publication Data
Names: Char, René, 1907–1988, author. / Carlson, Nancy Naomi, 1949– , translator.
Container of (expression): Char, René, 1907–1988. Marteau sans maître.
English Title: Hammer with no master / Le marteau sans maître
René Char ; translated by Nancy Naomi Carlson.
Other titles: Marteau sans maître / Tupelo Press poetry in translation.
Description: First paperback edition. / North Adams, Massachusetts : Tupelo Press, [2016]
Series: Tupelo Press poetry in translation / Includes bibliographical references.
Identifiers: LCCN 2016045097 / ISBN 9781936797899 (pbk. original : alk. paper)
Classification: LCC PQ2605.H3345 M313 2016 / DDC 841/.912—dc23

Cover and text designed by Josef Beery.
Cover: *Lightning strikes the Eiffel Tower on June 3, 1902.* Photograph by M. G. Loppé
from Wikimedia Commons, public domain.

First paperback edition: November 2016.

Tupelo Press
P.O. Box 1767, North Adams, Massachusetts 01247
Telephone: (413) 664–9611 / editor@tupelopress.org / www.tupelopress.org

Tupelo Press is an award-winning independent literary press that publishes fine fiction,
nonfiction, and poetry in books that are a joy to hold as well as read. Tupelo Press is a
registered 501(c)(3) nonprofit organization, and we rely on public support to carry out
our mission of publishing extraordinary work that may be outside the realm of the large
commercial publishers. Financial donations are welcome and are tax deductible.

**ART WORKS.**
arts.gov

*Supported in part by an award from the National Endowment for the Arts.*

Il faut aussi se souvenir de celui
qui oublie où mène le chemin.

We must also recall the one
who forgets where the road leads.

HERACLITUS

.

J'ai pleuré, j'ai sangloté à la vue
de cette demeure inaccoutumée.

I cried, I sobbed at the sight of
this strange dwelling place.

EMPEDOCLES

# Contents

Translator's Introduction    ix

ARSENAL | ARSENAL

i. La Torche du prodigue | The Prodigal's Torch    3

ii. Vérité continue | Continuous Truth    5

iii. Possible | Possible    7

iv. Tréma de l'émondeur | Pruner's Diaeresis    9

v. Robustes météores | Robust Meteors    11

vi. Transfuges | Renegades    13

vii. Masque de fer | Iron Mask    15

viii. Un levain barbare | Barbaric Leaven    17

ix. À l'horizon remarquable | On the Remarkable Horizon    19

x. Singulier | Singular    21

xi. Leçon sévère | Stern Lesson    23

xii. Bel édifice et les pressentiments |    25
Premonitions and Stately Building

xiii. La Rose violente | Violent Rose    27

xiv. Voici | Here    29

xv. L'Amour | Love    31

xvi. Sosie | Double    33

xvii. Dentelée | Jagged    35

xviii. Les Poumons | Lungs    37

ARTINE | ARTINE

Artine | Artine    41

## L'ACTION DE LA JUSTICE EST ÉTEINTE │ THE ACTION OF JUSTICE IS OVERTURNED

Poème │ Poem  49

Sommeil fatal │ Fatal Sleep  51

L'Oracle du grand oranger │ Oracle of the Great Orange Tree  53

La Manne de Lola Abba │ The Manna of Lola Abba  55

La Main de Lacenaire │ Lacenaire's Hand  57

Poètes │ Poets  59

L'Artisanat furieux │ Furious Craftsmanship  61

Les Messagers de la poésie frénétique │  63
Frenetic Poetry's Messengers

Les Soleils chanteurs │ Melodious Suns  65

Le Climat de chasse ou l'accomplissement de la poésie │  67
The Climate of Hunting or How Poems Are Made

L'Instituteur révoqué │ The Dismissed Instructor  69

Tu ouvres les yeux . . . │ You Open Your Eyes . . .  71


## POÈMES MILITANTS │ MILITANT POEMS

La Luxure │ Lust  75

Métaux refroidis │ Cooled Metals  77

Chaîne │ Chain  81

Les Asciens │ Men Without Shadows (Equator Dwellers)  83

Vivante demain │ Alive Tomorrow  85

Les Observateurs et les Rêveurs │ Observers and Dreamers  87

La Plaine │ The Plain  89

Confronts │ Confrontations  91

L'Historienne | The Historian     95

Sade, l'amour enfin sauvé de la boue du ciel,     97
cet héritage suffira aux hommes contre la famine |
Sade, Love Finally Saved from the Mud of the Sky,
this Legacy Will Suffice for Men Against Hunger

Le Supplice improvisé | Improvised Torture     99

Cruauté | Cruelty     101

Sommaire | Summary     103

Pour Mamouque | For Mamouque     105

Crésus | Croesus     107

Bourreaux de solitude | Hangmen of Solitude     111

Versant | Slope     113


ABONDANCE VIENDRA | ABUNDANCE WILL COME

L'Éclaircie | The Sunny Spell     117

Eaux-mères | The Mother Liquor     119

Les Rapports entre parasites |     127
Relations Between Parasites

Migration | Migration     131

Domaine | Domain     133

Intégration | Integrative     137

Devant soi | Ahead of You     139


Notes     141

Acknowledgments     144

# Translator's Introduction

René Char (1907–1988) was praised by Prime Minister Jacques
Chirac as "the greatest French poet of the twentieth century." His
friend and fellow writer Albert Camus wrote to him in a letter,
"There are few men today I admire for both language and character.
You are among them—the only contemporary poet who has dared
defend beauty, address it explicitly, and prove that it's something
we can fight for as much as for our daily bread. You go further
than anyone else, having rejected nothing."

*Le Marteau sans maître*, first published in 1934 and repre-
senting Char's most important early work, has never before been
translated in its entirety into English. Fred Chappell, former
Poet Laureate of North Carolina and winner of the Best Foreign
Book Prize from the Académie Française, has said that with the
publication of *Le Marteau sans maître*, Char's "essential poetic" was
formed and was "consistently affirmed and applied ever after."

Because of Char's dense style, thick with seemingly unrelated
images juxtaposed to one another, it was often challenging to sort
out the internal logic of each poem, and to find some thread of
continuity within and among the texts. Crucial, too, was the need
to hold back from making any semantic leaps for the reader; the
images had to stand on their own. Most often, the musicality of
the original French contributed to holding these pieces together,
and I made every effort to honor rhythmic and sonic patterns in
my translations.

I employed a "sound mapping" technique, where I identified
rhymes (slant and pure) and alliteration in the French. A sound
map for the first stanza of "Métaux refroidis" illustrates this
translation strategy.

| | |
|---|---|
| Métaux *refroidis* | *Cooled* Metals |
| *Touriste* des **crépuscules** | *Tourists* of dus**ks** |
| Dans tes parcs | In your par**ks** |
| Le **f**ilon de **f**oudre | **L**ightning's **l**ode |
| Se *perd* sous *terre* | **L**oses its way in the ground |
| Or **nocturne** | Nocturnal **gold** |

Notice the crisp "i" sound of "refroidis" and "touriste," the stressed "er" sound (with the throaty French "r") of "perd" and "terre," the alliteration of "f" in "filon" and "foudre," and the slant rhyming of the final word "nocturne" (and its forceful "u" sound) with "crépuscules" at the start of the poem. In addition, most of the French lines end with a stressed syllable. I then attempted to replicate similar patterns in English (though not necessarily exact sounds and placement), including the stressed "oo" sound of "cooled" and "tourists" and "loses," the alliteration of "l" in "lightning's," "lode," and "loses," the alliteration of "ks" in "dusks" and "parks," and the slant rhyming of the final word "gold" with the earlier "lode." I also made sure each line ended with a stressed syllable, to preserve the rhythm of the French.

*Le Marteau sans maître*, with dedications to André Breton and Paul Éluard, demonstrates Char's early ties with the Surrealist movement. Char had signed his name to *Le Manifeste du surréalisme*. However, although he valued poetry as a spontaneous activity, he renounced the Surrealists five years later, arguing that poetry must be free of limits imposed by any ideology or affiliation. Char not only translated his philosophical convictions into aesthetics, but also applied them to his life, fighting in the French underground during World War II for a liberated France, free from Nazi rule.

Char was influenced by the French poets Charles Baudelaire, Arthur Rimbaud, Stéphane Mallarmé, Guillaume Apollinaire, and

Paul Valéry, as well as by German poets Friedrich Hölderlin and
Rainer Maria Rilke. One can also see and hear the influences
of Friedrich Nietzsche and the ancient Greek philosopher
Heraclitus. Char achieved great public acclaim during his lifetime.
He collaborated with the visual artists Georges Braque, Henri
Matisse, Alberto Giacometti, and Pablo Picasso, and poems from
*Le Marteau sans maître* and others of his books were set to music
by composer Pierre Boulez. In English, such notables as William
Carlos Williams, Samuel Beckett, Richard Wilbur, James Wright,
John Ashbery, and W. S. Merwin—no doubt attracted to Char's
bold approach to themes of love, death, human existence, social
justice and freedom, the costs of war, wonder for the cosmos,
and the dignity of working people—have tried their hand at
translating the music and prophetic eloquence of individual Char
poems.

Now readers in English can experience for the first time ever
one of Char's most characteristic and influential volumes of poems
as a whole. Welcome to *Le Marteau sans maître*.

# Arsenal

## 1. La Torche du prodigue

Brûlé l'enclos en quarantaine
Toi nuage passé devant

Nuage de résistance
Nuage des cavernes
Entraîneur d'hypnose.

## I. The Prodigal's Torch

Burnt quarantined space
You passed cloud ahead

Cloud of resistance
Cloud of caves
Coach of hypnosis.

## II. VÉRITÉ CONTINUE

Le novateur de la lézarde
Tire la corde de tumulte

On mesure la profondeur
Aux contours émus de la cuisse

Le sang muet qui délivre
Tourne à l'envers les aiguilles
Remonte l'amour sans le lire.

## ii. Continuous Truth

The inventor of clefts
Takes chaos too far

We measure depth
From pressed contours of thigh

The mute and freeing blood
Turns needles upside down
Hoists back love without reading it aloud.

## III. POSSIBLE

Dès qu'il en eut la certitude
À coup de serrements de gorge
Il facilita la parole

Elle jouait sur les illustrés à quatre sous

Il parla comme on tue
Le fauve
Ou la pitié

Ses doigts touchèrent l'autre rive

Mais le ciel bascula
Si vite
Que l'aigle sur la montagne
Eut la tête tranchée.

## III. POSSIBLE

As soon as he knew for sure
By repeatedly squeezing his throat
He eased out the word

It played on the cheap comic strips

He spoke as one would kill
The wild beast
Or pity

His fingers touched the other shore

But the sky toppled over
So fast
That it cut off the head
Of the eagle perched on the mountain top.

## iv. Tréma de l'émondeur

Parce que le soleil faisait le paon sur le mur
Au lieu de voyager à dos d'arbre.

## iv. Pruner's Diaeresis

Because the peacock sun was strutting about on walls
Instead of traveling on backs of trees.

## v. Robustes météores

Dans le bois on écoute bouillir le ver
La chrysalide tournant au clair visage
Sa délivrance naturelle

Les hommes ont faim
De viandes secrètes d'outils cruels
Levez-vous bêtes à égorger
À gagner le soleil.

## v. Robust Meteors

In the wood we hear the worm boil
The pupa turning toward the clear face
Its natural means to be freed

Men are starved
For secret meats for cruel tools
Rise up you beasts of slaughter
To outrun the sun.

## vi. Transfuges

Sang enfin libérable
L'aérolithe dans la véranda
Respire comme une plante

L'esprit même du château fort
C'est le pont levis.

## VI. RENEGADES

Blood finally up for parole
The veranda's aerolite
Breathes like a plant

The fortified castle's very soul
Is the drawbridge.

## VII. Masque de fer

Ne tient pas qui veut sa rage secrète
Sans diplomatie.

## vii. Iron Mask

You can't hide rage
Without diplomacy.

## VIII. UN LEVAIN BARBARE

La bouche en chant
Dans un carcan
Comme à l'école
La première tête qui tombe.

## VIII. Barbaric Leaven

Mouth of refrains
In iron restraints
Just like in school
The first head to roll.

## IX. À L'HORIZON REMARQUABLE

Les grands chemins
Dorment à l'ombre de ses mains

Elle marche au supplice
Demain
Comme une traînée de poudre.

## ix. On the Remarkable Horizon

The great pathways
Sleep in her hands' shade

She heads for her torment
Tomorrow
Like a trail of gunpowder.

## x. Singulier

Passé ces trois mots elle ne dit plus rien
Elle mange à sa faim et plus
Haute est l'estime de ses draps

Nomade elle s'endort allongée sur ma bouche
Volume d'éther comme une passion
Délire à midi à minuit elle est fécondée dans
    le coma de l'amour arbitraire
La pièce de prédilection de l'oxygène.

## x. Singular

She says nothing else beyond these three words
She eats her fill and more
High is her sheets' esteem

Nomad, she falls asleep lying prone on my mouth
Volume of ether like passion
Frenzy at noon, at midnight she conceives
   in the coma of random love
Oxygen's room of choice.

## XI. Leçon sévère

Le saut iliaque accompli
L'attrait quitte la rêverie
L'amant baigné de tendresse est un levier
   mort
Les tournois infantiles
Sombrent dans la noce de la crasse
Le relais de la respiration

L'air était maternel
Les racines croissaient

Un petit nombre
A touché le jour
À la première classe
Que l'amour forme à l'étoile d'enfer
D'un sang jamais entendu.

## xi. Stern Lesson

The iliac leap achieved
The attraction leaves the daydream
The lover bathed with a tender regard is a dead
    lever
Childish tournaments
Sink into the wedding of grime
The relay of breaths

The air was maternal
The roots grew

A small number
Have reached the light
At the first class
That love forms at the hellish star
From a blood not the least bit understood.

## XII. Bel édifice et les pressentiments

J'écoute marcher dans mes jambes
La mer morte vagues par-dessus tête

Enfant la jetée-promenade sauvage
Homme l'illusion imitée

Des yeux purs dans les bois
Cherchent en pleurant la tête habitable.

## XII. Premonitions and Stately Building

I hear the dead sea move
In my legs, waves overhead

Child, the wild jetty-walk
Man, the echoed illusion

Pure eyes in the woods
Weeping seek the hospitable head.

## XIII. LA ROSE VIOLENTE

Oeil en transe miroir muet
Comme je m'approche je m'éloigne
Bouée au créneau

Tête contre tête tout oublier
Jusqu'au coup d'épaule en plein coeur
La rose violente
Des amants nuls et transcendants.

## XIII. VIOLENT ROSE

Eye in trance, mirror mute
As I approach I move away
Buoy in battlement gap

Head to head forgetting all
Until the shoulder jabs straight to the heart
The violent rose
Of lovers, transcendent and null.

## xiv. Voici

Voici l'écumeur de mémoire
Le vapeur des flaques mineures
Entouré de linges fumants
Étoile rose et rose blanche

Ô caresses savantes, ô lèvres inutiles!

## xiv. Here

Here, skimmer of memory's cream
Steamship of mined pools
Enclosed by linen's steamy reek
Rose star, white rose

O knowing caresses, o useless lips!

## xv. L'Amour

Être
Le premier venu.

## xv. Love

Being
The first to come.

## XVI. Sosie

Animal
À l'aide de pierres
Efface mes longues pelisses

Homme
Je n'ose pas me servir
Des pierres qui te ressemblent

Animal
Gratte avec tes ongles
Ma chair est d'une rude écorce

Homme
J'ai peur du feu
Partout où tu trouves

Animal
Tu parles
Comme un homme

Détrompe-toi
Je ne vais pas au bout de ton dénouement.

## XVI. DOUBLE

Animal
With the help of stones
Efface my long fur

Man
I dare not use
Stones that look like you

Animal
Scrape with your claws
My flesh is rough bark

Man
I'm afraid of flames
Wherever you're found

Animal
You speak
Like a man

Don't get me wrong
I'll not go to the tail end of your denouement.

## XVII. Dentelée

Baigneuse oublie-moi dans la mer
Qui délire et calme la foule.

## xvii. Jagged

Female swimmer, forget me in the sea
That raves, incoherent, and quiets the crowd.

## xviii. Les Poumons

L'apparition de l'arme à feu
La reconnaissance du ventre.

## XVIII. Lungs

The firearm arrives
The belly won't bite the hand that feeds it.

# ARTINE

*Au silence de celle qui laisse rêveur*

# ARTINE

*To the silence of one who lets us keep dreaming*

# ARTINE

*Dans le lit qu'on m'avait préparé il y avait: un animal sanguinolent et*
*meurtri, de la taille d'une brioche, un tuyau de plomb, une rafale de vent,*
*un coquillage glacé, une cartouche tirée, deux doigts d'un gant, une tache*
*d'huile; il n'y avait pas de porte de prison, il y avait le goût de l'amertume,*
*un diamant de vitrier, un cheveu, un jour, une chaise cassée, un ver à soie,*
*l'objet volé, une chaîne de pardessus, une mouche verte apprivoisée, une*
*branche de corail, un clou de cordonnier, une roue d'omnibus.*

Offrir au passage un verre d'eau à un cavalier lancé à bride abattue
sur un hippodrome envahi par la foule suppose, de part et d'autre, un
manque absolu d'adresse; Artine apportait aux esprits qu'elle visitait
cette sécheresse monumentale.

L'impatient se rendait parfaitement compte de l'ordre des rêves
qui hanteraient dorénavant son cerveau, surtout dans le domaine
de l'amour où l'activité dévorante se manifestait couramment en
dehors du temps sexuel; l'assimilation se développant, la nuit noire,
dans les serres bien closes.

Artine traverse sans difficulté le nom d'une ville. C'est le silence qui
détache le sommeil.

Les objets désignés et rassemblés sous le nom de nature-précise
font partie du décor dans lequel se déroulent les actes d'érotisme
des *suites fatales,* épopée quotidienne et nocturne. Les mondes imagi-
naires chauds qui circulent sans arrêt dans la campagne à l'époque
des moissons rendent l'oeil agressif et la solitude intolérable à celui

# ARTINE

*In the bed prepared for me lay a wounded animal covered in blood,*
*small as a bun, a lead pipe, a burst of wind, a glazed seashell, a spent*
*shotgun shell, two fingers of a glove, an oil stain; no prison door, but*
*yes, the taste of bitter resentment, a glazier's diamond, one hair, one*
*day, a broken chair, a silkworm, the stolen object, an overcoat's chain,*
*a tame green fly, a coral branch, a cobbler's nail, a wheel from a bus.*

To offer a glass of water to a horseman hurtling by on a race-track overrun by the crowd implies a complete lack of skill on both sides; Artine brought this epic drought to the minds to which she appeared.

Impatient, he was very well aware of the order of dreams which would haunt his brain from here on, mainly in love's domain whose all-consuming pursuits usually appeared at non-sexual times—assimilation unfolding in pitch-black dark, in greenhouses tightly closed.

Artine easily passes through the name of a town. Silence detaches sleep.

The items gathered and arranged under the name of *nature-précise* are part of the scene where erotic acts with *fatal conse-quences*—a daily epic—unfold each night. The hot imaginary worlds that circulate nonstop in the countryside during the harvest season give rise to unbearable loneliness, violent eyes in the

qui dispose du pouvoir de destruction. Pour les extraordinaires bouleversements il est tout de même préférable de s'en remettre entièrement à eux.

L'état de léthargie qui précédait Artine apportait les éléments indispensables à la projection d'impressions saisissantes sur l'écran de ruines flottantes: édredon en flammes précipité dans l'insondable gouffre de ténèbres en perpétual mouvement.

Artine gardait en dépit des animaux et des cyclones une intarissable fraîcheur. À la promenade, c'était la transparence absolue.

À beau surgir au milieu de la plus active dépression l'appareil de la beauté d'Artine, les esprits curieux demeurent des esprits furieux, les esprits indifférents des esprits extrêmement curieux.

Les apparitions d'Artine dépassaient le cadre de ces contrées du sommeil, où le *pour* et le *pour* sont animés d'une égale et meurtrière violence. Elles évoluaient dans les plis d'une soie brûlante peuplée d'arbres aux feuilles de cendre.

La voiture à chevaux lavée et remise à neuf l'emportait presque toujours sur l'appartement tapissé de salpêtre lorsqu'il s'agissait d'accueillir durant une soirée interminable la multitude des ennemis mortels d'Artine. Le visage de bois mort était particulièrement odieux. La course haletante de deux amants au hasard des grands chemins devenait tout à coup une distraction suffisante pour permettre au drame de se dérouler, derechef, à ciel ouvert.

one who wields destructive force. Still, for extraordinary times of upheaval it's best to completely rely on them.

The lethargic state preceding Artine provided the means for projecting startling impressions onto the screen of floating ruins: burning eiderdown cast into the bottomless depths of perpetually moving shadows.

Despite beasts and cyclones, Artine retained an endless freshness. On strolls, this was total transparency.

From the most active depression, Artine's aggregate beauty may spring, but curious minds remain furious; neutral minds become extremely curious.

Artine's apparitions went past the border of those countries of sleep where the *for* and the *for* are imbued with an equal and murderous violence. They evolved in the pleats of a burning silk planted with trees with leaves of ash.

Washed and refurbished, the horse-drawn carriage nearly always prevailed over the room with saltpeter-papered walls and the never-ending evenings greeting Artine's  many mortal enemies. The dead-wood face was especially hard to take. The breathless race of two lovers at random along the highways became, all at once, enough entertainment to let it play out again in the open air.

Quelquefois une manoeuvre maladroite faisait tomber sur la gorge d'Artine une tête qui n'était pas la mienne. L'énorme bloc de soufre se consumait alors lentement, sans fumée, présence en soi et immobilité vibrante.

Le livre ouvert sur les genoux d'Artine était seulement lisible les jours sombres. À intervalles irréguliers les héros venaient apprendre les malheurs qui allaient à nouveau fondre sur eux, les voies multiples et terrifiantes dans lesquelles leur irréprochable destinée allait à nouveau s'engager. Uniquement soucieux de la Fatalité, ils étaient pour la plupart d'un physique agréable. Ils se déplaçaient avec lenteur, se montraient peu loquaces. Ils exprimaient leurs désirs à l'aide de larges mouvements de tête imprévisibles. Ils paraissaient en outre s'ignorer totalement entre eux.

Le poète a tué son modèle.

Sometimes a clumsy movement caused a head other than mine to sink on Artine's breast. The enormous sulfur block slowly burned away without smoke, presence in self and vibrating stillness.

The open book in Artine's lap could only be read on overcast days. At irregular intervals, heroes would come to learn the afflictions about to befall them once more, the many and dreadful paths in which their faultless fate would enlist anew. Only concerned with Destiny, they mostly looked pleasant. They moved about slowly, were men of few words. They expressed their desires through broad, unpredictable movements of heads. What's more, they seemed quite unaware of each other.

The poet has slain his model.

# L'Action de la justice est éteinte

*à André Breton*

# The Action of Justice Is Overturned

*for André Breton*

## Poème

Deux êtres également doués d'une grande loyauté sexuelle font un jour la preuve que leurs représentations respectives pendant l'orgasme diffèrent totalement les unes des autres: représentations graphiques continuelles chez l'un, représentations chimériques périodiques chez l'autre. Elles diffèrent au point que les nappes de visions au fur et à mesure de leur formation obtiennent le pouvoir d'engendrer une série de conflits mortels d'origine minérale mystérieuse, constituant dans le règne une nouveauté dont déni d'amour radicalement insoluble semble l'expression naturelle.

« Ma salive sur ton sexe,» crie l'homme à la femme, «c'est encore ton sang qui échappe au contrôle de mes mains. »

« Le vent qui se lève dans ta bouche a déjà traversé le ciel de nos réveils. Je n'aperçois pas davantage la ligne capitale dans le vol de l'aigle, grand directeur de conscience. »

Les amants virent s'ouvrir, au cours de cette phase nouvelle de leur existence, une ère de justice bouleversante. Ils flétrirent le crime passionnel, rendirent le viol au hasard, multiplièrent l'attentat à la pudeur, sources authentiques de la poésie. L'ampleur démesurée de leurs mouvements, passage de l'espoir dans l'être indifférent au désespoir dans l'être aimé, exprima la fatalité acquise. Dans le domaine irréconciliable de la surréalité, l'homme privilégié ne pouvant être que la proie gracieuse de sa dévorante raison de vivre: l'amour.

## Poem

Two people, both endowed with great sexual honesty, one day get proof that their mental pictures during orgasm vastly differ: continuous, graphic pictures with one; periodic, chimeric scenes with the other. They differ to such an extent that the layers of visions, as they are formed, have the power to bring about a series of mortal disputes of mysterious mineral origin, giving rise in the reign to a change where denial of completely insoluble love seems the natural expression.

"My saliva on your sex," shouts the man to the woman, "is still your blood that evades the control of my hands."

"The wind that begins to blow in your mouth has already crossed the sky of our awakenings. I no longer perceive the key line in the eagle's flight, great director of consciousness."

During this new phase of their existence, the lovers saw the start of an era of justice turned upside down. They withered crimes of passion, returned rape to chance, increased indecent assaults, genuine sources of poetry. The huge scope of their movements—hope passing through the one unmoved by the loved one's despair—expressed the accepted fate. In surrealism's realm that cannot be reconciled, privileged man can only be the gracious prey of his ravenous reason for living: love.

## Sommeil fatal

Les animaux à tête de navire cernent le visage de la femme que j'aime. Les herbes de montagne se fanent sous l'accalmie des paupières. Ma mémoire réalise sans difficulté ce qu'elle croit être l'acquis de ses rêves les plus désespérés, tandis qu'à portée de ses miroirs continue à couler l'eau introuvable. Et la pensée de cendres?

## Fatal Sleep

The beasts at the head of the ship wreathe the face of the woman I love. Mountain herbs fade under the stillness of eyelids. My memory easily becomes what it believes to be the gain of its most hopeless dreams, while water that cannot be found continues to flow in its mirrors' scope. And the thought of ash?

## L'Oracle du grand oranger

L'homme qui emporte l'évidence sur ses épaules
Garde le souvenir des vagues dans les entrepôts de sel.

## ORACLE OF THE GREAT ORANGE TREE

The man who carries evidence on his shoulders
Keeps the memory of waves in the warehouse of salt.

## La Manne de Lola Abba

*L'étroite croix noire dans les herbes portait: Lola Abba, 1912–1929.*

*Juillet. La nuit. Cette jeune fille morte noyée avait joué dans des herbes semblables, s'y était couchée, peut-être pour aimer . . . Lola Abba, 1912–1929. Un oubli difficile: une inconnue pourtant.*

*Deux semaines plus tard, une jeune fille s'est présentée à la maison: ma mère a-t-elle besoin d'une bonne? Je ne sais. Je ne puis répondre.—Revenez?—Impossible.—Alors, veuillez laisser votre nom?—Elle écrit quelquechose.—Adieu, mademoiselle. Le jeune corps s'engage dans l'allée du parc, disparaît derrière les arbres mouillés (il a fini de pleuvoir). Je me penche sur le nom: Lola Abba! Je cours, j'appelle . . . Pourquoi personne, personne à présent?*

*J'ai gardé tes sombres habits, très pauvres. Voici ton poème:*

Que je me peigne, dis-tu, comme passé à la terre la couronne d'amour.

Le charbon n'est pas sorti de prison qu'on disperse ses cendres violettes.

Ceux qui ont vraiment le goût du néant brûlent leurs vêtements avant de mourir.

Et si la cueillette des champignons, après la pluie, a quelque chose de macabre, ce n'est pas moi qui m'en plaindrai.

## The Manna of Lola Abba

*The narrow black cross in the grass was inscribed: Lola Abba, Age 17.*

*July. The night. This dead, drowned girl had been playing in similar grass, maybe she had been lying there, perhaps to be loved . . . Lola Abba, Age 17. Hard to forget, yet unknown.*

*Two weeks later, a girl appeared at the house: is my mother in need of a maid? I don't know. I can't answer. "Come back?" "Impossible." "Then will you please leave your name?" She writes something down. "Farewell, miss." The young body steps onto the path of the park, disappearing behind the wet trees (the rain has stopped). I examine her writing: Lola Abba! I run, I call . . . Why nobody, nobody now?*

*I have kept your somber clothing, frayed and old. Here is your poem:*

Let me comb my hair, you say, as the wreath of love left to the earth.

The charcoal is still confined to jail, yet its violet ashes are scattered.

Those with truly a taste for the void burn their clothes before they die.

And if gathering mushrooms after the rain is macabre somehow, I won't be the one to complain.

## La Main de Lacenaire

Les mondes éloquents ont été perdus.

## LACENAIRE'S HAND

Eloquent worlds have been lost.

## Poètes

La tristesse des illettrés dans les ténèbres des bouteilles
L'inquiétude imperceptible des charrons
Les pièces de monnaie dans la vase profonde

Dans les nacelles de l'enclume
Vit le poète solitaire
Grande brouette des marécages.

## Poets

Sadness of those unschooled in the bottles' gloom
Imperceptible fear of wheelwrights
Coins in deep ooze

In the anvil's hollows
The poet lives apart
Great wheelbarrow of bogs.

## L'Artisanat furieux

La roulotte rouge au bord du clou
Et cadavre dans le panier
Et chevaux de labours dans le fer à cheval
Je rêve la tête sur la pointe de mon couteau
   le Pérou.

# FURIOUS CRAFTSMANSHIP

Gypsy caravan—red on the edge of the nail
And dead body in basket
And workhorses in horseshoe
I dream my head on the tip of my knife
    Peru.

## LES MESSAGERS DE LA POÉSIE FRÉNÉTIQUE

Les soleils fainéants se nourrissent de méningite
Ils descendent les fleuves du moyen âge
Dorment dans les crevasses des rochers
Sur un lit de copeaux et de loupe
Ils ne s'écartent pas de la zone des tenailles pourries
Comme les aérostats de l'enfer.

# Frenetic Poetry's Messengers

Lazy suns feed off meningitis
They ride down rivers from the Middle Ages
Sleep in the fissures of rocks
On a bed of wooden chips and gnarls
They don't stray from the rotted pincers' zone
Like hot-air balloons of hell.

## LES SOLEILS CHANTEURS

Les disparitions inexplicables

Les accidents imprévisibles

Les malheurs un peu gros

Les catastrophes de tout ordre

Les cataclysmes qui noient et qui carbonisent

Le suicide considéré comme un crime

Les dégénérés intraitables

Ceux qui s'entourent la tête d'un tablier de forgeron

Les naïfs de première grandeur

Ceux qui descendent le cercueil de leur mère au
    fond d'un puits

Les cerveaux incultes

Les cervelles de cuir

Ceux qui hivernent à l'hôpital et que leur linge
    éclaté enivre encore

La mauve des prisons

L'ortie des prisons

La pariétaire de prisons

Le figuier allaiteur de ruines

Les silencieux incurables

Ceux qui canalisent l'écume du monde souterrain

Les amoureux dans l'extase

Les poètes terrassiers

Les magiciens à l'épi

Règnent température clémente autour des fauves
    embaumeurs du travail.

## MELODIOUS SUNS

Inexplicable deaths
Unpredictable accidents
Mishaps a bit out of hand
Disasters of every kind
Cataclysmic floods and fires
Suicide viewed as a crime
Determined degenerates
Those who wrap a blacksmith's smock
    around their head
Guileless ones of the first order
Those who lower their mother's casket
    down to the depths of a well
Uncultivated minds
Leather brains
Those who winter in hospital wards and whose
    torn laundry still makes them drunk
Prison mauve
Prison nettle
Prison wall lichwort
Fig tree wet nurse of ruins
Incurable silent ones
Those who canalize foam from the underground world
Lovers in ecstasy
Poets who excavate
Wizards of sprigs
Reign—pleasant weather for sweaty embalmers
    of work.

## Le Climat de chasse ou l'Accomplissement de la poésie

Mon pur sanglot suivi de son venin : le cerveau de mon amour courtisé par les tessons de bouteilles.

Ah! que dans la maison des éclipses, celle qui domine, en se retirant, fasse l'obscurité. On finira bien par retenir la direction prise par certaines orages dans les rapides du crépuscule.

Dans l'amour, il y a encore l'immobilité, ce sexe géant.

Tard dans la nuit nous sommes allés cueillir les fruits indispensables à mes songes de mort : les figues violettes.

Les archaïques carcasses de chevaux en forme de baignoire passent et s'estompent. Seule la classe de l'engrais parle et rassure.

Quand je partirai longuement dans un monde sans aspect, tous les loisirs de la vapeur au chevet du grand oranger.

Dans mes étisies extrêmes, une jeune fille à taille d'amanite apparaît, égorge un coq, puis tombe dans un sommeil léthargique, tandis qu'à quelques mètres de son lit coulent tout un fleuve et ses périls. Ambassade déportée.

> Défense de l'amour violence
> Asphyxie instant du diamant
> Paralysie douceur errante.

# THE CLIMATE OF HUNTING OR
# HOW POEMS ARE MADE

My pure sob overcome by its venom: my love's brain wooed by shards of glass.

Ah! May the one who rules in the house of eclipses, retreating, bring on the darkness. We'll do well, in the end, to keep in mind the direction some storms take in the rapids of dusk.

In love, there is still the stillness, this giant organ of sex.

Late at night we went to gather the fruit essential to my dreams of death: purple figs.

Archaic horse carcasses shaped like bathtubs pass and fade away. Only the class of manure speaks, reassures.

When I finally take my leave for a faceless world, all the pastimes of steam at the foot of the big orange tree.

In my extreme feverish states, a young woman, toadstool-sized, appears, slits the throat of a rooster, then falls into deep, lethargic sleep, while some meters away from her bed flows a whole river filled with perils. Embassy carried off course.

> Love's defense violence
> The diamond's insistent asphyxia
> Paralysis wandering ease.

## L'Instituteur révoqué

Trois personnages d'une banalité éprouvée s'abordent à des titres poétiques divers (du feu, je vous prie, quelle heure avez-vous, à combien de lieues la prochaine ville?), dans un paysage indifférent et engagent une conversation dont les échos ne nous parviendront jamais. Devant vous, le champ de dix hectares dont je suis le laboureur, le sang secret et la pierre catastrophique. Je ne vous laisse rien à penser.

## The Dismissed Instructor

Three fictional speakers of proven banality greet each other with varied poetic devices (*please, got a light, how many leagues to the closest town, what's the time?*). In an average locale they engage in chitchat whose echoes will never come close to our ears. Before you, the metered field of ten hectares. I am its plowman, its secret blood, its calamitous stone. I leave you nothing to fill your mind.

## TU OUVRES LES YEUX . . .

Tu ouvres les yeux sur la carrière d'ocre inexploitable
Tu bois dans un épieu l'eau souterraine
Tu es pour la feuille hypnotisée dans l'espace
À l'approche de l'invisible serpent
O ma diaphane digitale!

## You Open Your Eyes . . .

You open your eyes to an ocher quarry that cannot be mined
You drink in speared underground streams
You are under the spell of the hanging leaf
Stirred by the snake's muted approach
O my translucent foxglove!

## Poèmes Militants

*à Gilbert Lely*

## Militant Poems

*for Gilbert Lely*

## La Luxure

L'aigle voit de plus en plus s'effacer les pistes de la
　mémoire gelée
L'étendue de solitude rend à peine visible la proie filante
À travers chacune des régions
Où l'on tue où l'on est tué sans contrainte
Proie insensible
Projetée indistinctement
En deçà du désir et au delà de la mort

Le rêveur embaumé dans sa camisole de force
Entouré d'outils temporaires
Figures aussitôt évanouies que composées
Leur révolution célèbre l'apothéose de la vie déclinante
La disparition progressive des parties léchées
La chute des torrents dans l'opacité des tombeaux
Les sueurs et les malaises annonciateurs du feu central
L'univers enfin de toute sa poitrine athlétique
Nécropole fluvial
Après le déluge des sourciers

Ce fanatique des nuages
A le pouvoir surnaturel
De déplacer sur des distances considérables
Les paysages habituels
De rompre l'harmonie agglomérée
De rendre méconnaissables les lieux funèbres
Au lendemain des meurtres productifs
Sans que la conscience originelle
Se couvre du purificateur glissement de terrain.

# Lust

The eagle sees frozen memory's tracks grow more and more faint
The stretch of solitude makes it hard to see the darting prey
Across each of the regions
Where one freely kills or gets killed
Cold-hearted prey
Indistinctly projected
On this side of desire and the other side of death

The dreamer embalmed in his straightjacket
Surrounded with short-lived tools
Figures faded as soon as they're composed
Their revolution lauds the high point of life in decline
The progressive extinction of licked parts
Torrential cascades in opaqueness of tombs
Sweats and malaise announcing the central fire
The universe finally with full athletic chest
Fluvial necropolis
After the deluge of water-diviners

This fanatic of clouds
Endowed with super powers
Displaces commonplace landscapes
Over considerable space
Disrupts agglomerate harmony
Makes it impossibly hard to recognize mournful crime scenes
The day after productive homicides
Without a purging landslide
That hides what first is known.

## Métaux refroidis

Touriste des crépuscules
Dans tes parcs
Le filon de foudre
Se perd sous terre
Or nocturne

Habitant des espaces nubiles de l'amour
Le vert-de-gris des bêches va fleurir

Libérateur du cercle
Justicier des courants inhumains
Après le silex le gypse
La tête lointaine nébuleuse
Minuscule dans sa matrice glacée
Cette tête ne vaut pas
Le bras de fer qui la défriche
La pierre qui la fracasse
Le marécage qui l'enlise
Le lac qui la noie
La cartouche de dynamite qui la pulvérise
Cette tête ne vaut pas
La paille qui la mange
Le crime qui l'honore
Le monument qui la souille
Le délire qui la dénonce
Le scandale qui la rappelle
Le pont qui la traverse
La mémoire qui la rejette

# COOLED METALS

Tourist of dusks
In your parks
Lightning's lode
Loses its way in the ground
Nocturnal gold

Dweller of nubile spaces of love
The verdigris of spades will bloom

The one who sets the circle free
Robin Hood of inhuman currents
After flint, gypsum
The nebulous distant head
Minute in its frozen mold
This head isn't worth
The iron arm that tills its soil
The stone that smashes it in
The marsh that makes it sink
The lake that drowns it
The dynamite cartridge that blows it to bits
This head isn't worth
The straw by which it's consumed
The crime that holds it in high regard
The statue by which it's defaced
The delirium by which it's exposed
The uproar that calls it back
The bridge that spans it
The memory that casts it out

Introuvable sommeil
Arbre couché sur ma poitrine
Pour détourner les sources rouges
Devrai-je te suivre longtemps
Dans ta croissance éternelle?

Sleep that cannot be found
Tree stretched across my chest
To reroute red springs
Will I have to follow you for long
In your never ending growth?

# CHAÎNE

Le grand bûcher des alliances

Sous le spiral ciel d'échec

C'est l'hiver en barque pourrie

Des compagnons solides aux compagnes liquides

Des lits de mort sous les écorces

Dans les profondeurs vacantes de la terre

Les arcs forgent un nouveau nombre d'ailes

Les labours rayonnants adorent les guérisseurs détrempés

Sur la paille des fatalistes

L'écume d'astre coule tout allumée

Il n'y a pas d'absence irremplaçable.

# CHAIN

Great wood pyre of leagues
Under the spiral sky of defeat
It is winter's rotted skiff
From solid comrades to liquid lovers
Deathbeds beneath the trees
In the vacant depths of the earth
Arches forge a fresh supply of wings
Tilled fields radiate, worship sweat-drenched healers
On the straw of those who believe in fate
Flows the foam of ignited stars
There is no absence that cannot be replaced.

## Les Asciens

Découvre-toi la fraîcheur commence à tomber
Le salut méprisable est dans l'un des tiroirs de nos
    passions
L'expérience de l'amour
Glanée à la mosaïque des délires
Oriente notre devenir
Nous sommes visiblement présents
En surface
Pour le baiser de fausse route
Nous écrasons les derniers squelettes vibrants du
    parc idéal
D'un bout à l'autre de la distance hors mémoire
Nous apparaissons comme les végétaux complets
Envahisseurs du nouvel âge primitif
Sujet au royaume de la pariétaire profonde
Pour une période de jeunesse
Nous regardons couler dans les veines des chairs
    volatiles
Les fleurs microscopiques de la marée
En nous
La vie le mouvement la paralysie la mort est un
    voyage par eau comme la barre d'acier
Les lettres de la Table sont gravées sur une plaque
    publique clouée
Nous touchons au nœud du métal
Qui donne la mort
Sans laisser de trace.

## Men Without Shadows
## (Equator Dwellers)

Take off your hat    coolness is starting to fall
The repugnant salute is in one of the drawers
    of our passions
Love affairs
Gleaned from delirium's mosaic
Orient our fate
We are clearly here
On the surface
Poised for the wrong turn's kiss
We crush vibrant skeletons    last ones of the
    ideal park
From one end to the other beyond memory's range
We appear like complete plants
Invading the new primitive age
Subject in deep lichwort's realm
For a youthful stage
We watch microscopic blooms of the tide
Flow in the veins of volatile flesh
Within us
Life    movement    paralysis    death
    a journey by sea like the steel bar
The Table's letters are carved on a nailed
    public slab
We touch the metal knot
Which kills
Without leaving a trace.

## Vivante demain

Par la grande échappée du mur
Je t'ai reçue votive des mains de l'hiver

Je te regardais traversant les anneaux de sable des
    cuirasses
Comme la génération des mélancoliques le préau des jeux

Sur l'herbe de plomb
Sur l'herbe de mâchefer
Sur l'herbe jamais essoufflée
Hors de laquelle la ressemblance des brûlures avec leur
    fatalité n'est jamais parfaite
Faisons l'amour.

## Alive Tomorrow

Through the gap in the wall
I took you in—votive—from winter's hands

I watched you crossing the armored waves of sand—
Generation of brooders crossing the playground

On leaden grass
On grass of slag
On grass never gasping for breath
Past where degrees of burn and their fate
   are never exactly paired
Let us make love.

## LES OBSERVATEURS ET LES RÊVEURS

*à Maurice Blanchard*

Avant de rejoindre les nomades
Les séducteurs allument les colonnes de pétrole
Pour dramatiser les récoltes

Demain commenceront les travaux poétiques
Précédés du cycle de la mort volontaire
Le règne de l'obscurité a coulé la raison le diamant
 dans la mine

Mères éprises des mécènes du dernier soupir
Mères excessives
Toujours à creuser le coeur massif
Sur vous passera indéfiniment le frisson des fougères
 des cuisses embaumées
On vous gagnera
Vous vous coucherez

Seuls aux fenêtres des fleuves
Les grands visages éclairs
Rêvent qu'il n'y a rien de périssable
Dans leur paysage carnassier.

## OBSERVERS AND DREAMERS
### *for Maurice Blanchard*

Before rejoining the nomads
Seducers ignite pillars of oil
To dramatize reapings of what was sown

Tomorrow poetic toil begins
Led by the cycle of death by free will
The reign of darkness engulfing reason, diamond
    inside the mine

Mothers in love with patrons of the last breath
Mothers prone to excess
Always tilling the massive heart
Through you will endlessly pass shivering ferns
    of embalmed thighs
You will be won
You will go to bed

Alone at the windows of rivers
Great faces filled with light
Dream there is nothing that dies
In their flesh-eating tableau.

## La Plaine

Vous contemplez, ô Majesté
L'effondrement des rieurs autour de la cuve
    de goudron
L'éternité
C'est l'insistant reflet amoureux de votre corps
Dans le chaos de la précision
Je vous ai soustraite
Aux planches de dégoût des verdicts universels
La fente boréale détermine les rêves
Voici l'aile prophétique du sphinx linceul pour
    l'inconstante.

## THE PLAIN

You behold, o Majesty
The fall of those who laugh around the vat
   of tar
Eternity—
The steadfast reflection in love with your body
In precision's chaos
I shielded you
From generic verdicts' boards of disgust
The boreal cleft determines dreams
Here's the prophetic wing of the Sphinx—
   shroud for you, the fickle one.

## CONFRONTS

*à Marcel Fourrier*

Dans le juste milieu de la roche et du sable de l'eau et du feu
    des cris et du silence universels
Parfait comme l'or
Le spectacle de ciment de la Beauté clouée
Chantage

Dehors
La terre s'ouvre
L'homme est tué
L'air se referme

Les notions de l'indépendance sucrent au goût des
    oppresseurs le sang des opprimés
Les fainéants crépitent avec les flammes du bûcher
C'est la transmutation des richesses harmonieuses
Le langage des porteurs de scapulaire: «Au crépuscule
À l'heure où les poissons viennent en troupeau
Respirer à la surface de la mer
Invariablement
La main à cinq hameçons
La main divine
Cueille le fruit du sel»

Hypothétique lecteur
Mon confident désœuvré
Qui a partagé ma panique

## CONFRONTATIONS
### *for Marcel Fourrier*

In the happy medium found between rock and sand,
    water and fire, universal silence and screams
Perfect as gold
The sight of cement with Beauty pinned
Blackmail

Outside
The earth opens
Man is killed
The air reseals

For those who oppress, ideas of autonomy sweeten
    the blood's taste of those oppressed
Slackers crackle with flames of the pyre
Transmutation of riches in harmony
Language of those draped with scapulars: "Dusk,
At the hour when fish flock in shoals
To breathe on the surface of waves
In every case
The hand with five hooks
The divine hand
Gathers the fruit of salt"

Hypothetical reader
My idle confidant
Sharing my dread

Quand la bêche s'est refusée à mordre le lin
Puisse un mirage d'abreuvoirs sur l'atlas des déserts
Aggraver ton désir de prendre congé
Les vivants parlent aux morts de médecine salvatrice
    de tireur de hasard à la roue de la raison
Les armées solides sont liquides après la chimie
    des oiseaux
Les yeux les moins avides embrassent à la fois le
    panorama et les ressources de l'île
Plante souple dans un sol rude

Mais voici le progrès

Les mondes en transformation appartiennent aux poètes
    carnassiers
Les distractions meurtrières aux rêveurs qui les imaginet
À l'esprit de fonder le pessimisme en dormant
Au temps de la jeunesse du corps
Pour voir grandir
La chair flexible et douce
Au-dessus des couleurs
À travers les cristaux des consciences inflexibles
Au chevet de la violence dilapidée
Dans l'animation de l'amour
Lorsqu'elle passera devant le soleil
Peut-être le dernier simple incarnera la lumière.

When the spade refused to bite the flax
May a mirage of watering holes on the atlas of
   desert sands
Increase your desire to take leave
The living speak to the dead about life-saving medical science
   from shooters of chance at the wheel of reason
Solid armies turn liquid after the chemistry of birds
The least greedy eyes embrace panoramic views and the
   island's resources, both at the same time
Pliable plant in a hard soil

But here is progress

Transforming worlds belong to carnivorous poets
Deadly distractions to dreamers who dream
   them alive
The mind must sleep to create pessimistic beliefs
In the time of the body's youth
To see grow
Supple and soft flesh
Above the hues
Through crystals of rigid consciences
At bedsides of violence dispersed
In the true animation of love
When it overtakes the sun
Perhaps the simple last one will incarnate the light.

## L'Historienne

Celle qui coule l'or à travers la corne
Qui crève la semence
Mange aux pôles
Dort au feu de terre

L'expression d'épouvante du visage du carrier
Précipité dans la chaux vive
Asphyxié sous les yeux d'une femme
—Son dos aux veines palpitantes
Ses lèvres de fleuve
Sa jouissance grandiose

Tout ce qui se détache convulsivement de l'unité
　　du monde
De la masse débloquée par la simple poussée d'une
　　enfant
Et fond sur nous à toute vitesse
Nous qui ne confondons pas les actes à vivre et
　　les actes vécus
Qui ne savons pas désirer en priant
Obtenir en simulant
Qui voyons la nuit au défaut de l'épaule de la
　　dormeuse
Le jour dans l'épanouissement du plaisir

Dans un ciel d'indifférence
L'oiseau rouge des métaux
Vole soucieux d'embellir l'existence
La mémoire de l'amour regagne silencieusement
　　sa place
Parmi les poussières.

# The Historian

She who casts gold through the horn
That punctures the seed
Eats at the poles
Sleeps in the earth's fire

Terrified look on the quarryman's face
Hurled into quicklime
Asphyxiated right in front of a woman's eyes
—His back with quivering veins
His lips of river
His exquisite climax

All that convulsively breaks away from the oneness
    of the world
Released from the mass by the simple push of a
    child
And swoops down on us at full speed
We who don't confuse acts to be lived and
    acts already lived
Don't know how to desire through prayer
Nor procure through pretense
And at night over the sleeping girl's shoulder
    see
The day flowering in full delight

In an indifferent sky
The red bird of metals
Flies anxious to beautify daily life
The memory of love regains in silence
    its place
As part of the dusts.

## SADE, L'AMOUR ENFIN SAUVÉ DE LA BOUE DU CIEL, CET HÉRITAGE SUFFIRA AUX HOMMES CONTRE LA FAMINE

*à Maurice Heine*

Le pur sang ravi à la roseraie

Frôleuse mentale en flambeau

Si juteuse le crin flatté

L'odorat surmené à proximité d'une colonie de délices

Hèle les désirs écartés

Empire de la rose déshabillée

Comme gel sous l'eau noire sommeil fatal crapaud.

## SADE, LOVE FINALLY SAVED FROM THE MUD OF THE SKY, THIS LEGACY WILL SUFFICE FOR MEN AGAINST HUNGER

*for Maurice Heine*

The pure blood overjoyed at the rose garden

Torched mental temptress

So juicy the stroked tail of a horse

Sense of smell overworked near a swarm of delights

Hails discarded lust

The undressed rose reigns

As ice beneath black water, the fatal sleep flaw.

## Le Supplice improvisé

Penchante

Détournée de lavures

En avance d'un jour néfaste

Elle dort dans une corbeille d'osier

Comme une chemise glacée

Il faut beaucoup de froid et beaucoup d'ombre

Pour obtenir qu'elle s'éloigne

Talon maître des étincelles

Découvre le gage misérable

Laisse-moi me convaincre de l'éphémère qui enchantait
    hier ses yeux

Sommeil d'amour ô sommeil magnétique

—L'arnica au soleil et le lit au matin—

Je ne subis pas le sentiment de la privation.

## IMPROVISED TORTURE

Slanting
Detoured from kitchen swills
In advance of an ill-fated day
She sleeps in a wicker basket
Like an icy shirt
Much cold and shade are required
To get her to move away
Master heel of sparks
Reveal the pitiful pawn
Let me find proof of ephemera that yesterday
    thrilled her eyes
Sleep of love o magnetic sleep—
Arnica blooms in the sun and the bed at dawn—
I don't suffer from any lack.

## Cruauté

L'abondant été de l'homme
Que celui qui suivit l'établissement par ses soins
    des premières dénaturations
En faisant la part de l'aveuglement
Piétinée la croûte tiède pulvérisé l'avorton
Celui qui éclaire ne sera pas éclairé
Contemple sans pouvoir l'achever la merveille
    agonisante
Le portail poussé tu t'abats

Nous subissons la loi corruptrice du Borgne
Les brûlantes détresses locales sont le fruit de nos
    glandes
Nous nous galvanisons dans les cendres qui nous
    ont vomi
Comme si les excroissances de chair contenaient
    des dépôts malsains
Instruments de perfection types précis
Nous sommes les pieds d'une grandeur sans
    pareille

Les peuples danseurs obnubilés par le sentiment
    de plénitude
Après l'exaltation
Se dévêtent de la substance de jouir
Retournent à la projection permanente
Alors les fumées coriaces construisent des postes
    dans le vent
La décomposition jamais surprise par la justesse
    du projectile
Va dans le cadavre
Accomplir sa besogne massive de couleuvre
Jusqu'à nous.

## CRUELTY

The abundant summer of man
The very one that followed the first unnatural changes
    established under his watch
By taking blindness into account
The warm crust trampled, the weakling smashed
The one who enlightens will not be enlightened
Gaze upon the dying marvel you cannot completely destroy
The portal pushed, you collapse

We endure the corrupt law of the One-Eyed
Localized burning distress is the fruit of our glands
We galvanize ourselves in the ashes that spewed us up
As if outgrowths of flesh contained toxic dregs
Tools of perfection, precise types
We are the feet of a greatness without peer

The dancing masses obsessed by sensations of plenitude
After elation
Strip themselves of the stuff of delight
Revert to projection that's permanent
Then stubborn smoke constructs posts in the wind
Decay never caught off guard by projectiles' precision
Enters the corpse
To complete its massive task of a garter snake
Reaching even up to us.

## Sommaire

L'homme criblé de lésions par les infiltrations
   considéra son désespoir et le trouva inférieur
Autour de lui les règnes n'arrêtaient pas de s'ennoblir
Comme la délicate construction gicle du solstice
   de la charrette saute au cœur sans portée
Il pressentit les massifs du denouement
Et stratège
S'engagea dans le raccourci fascinateur
Qui ne le conduisit nulle part

Au terme de la bourbe insociable
Le sphérique des respirations pénétra dans la paix.

## SUMMARY

The man riddled with lesions caused by infiltrates
    judged his despair and found it second-rate
All around him kingdoms kept ennobling themselves
As the fragile construction spurts out of the solstice,
    it jumps from the cart to the boundless heart
He sensed the mountain heights of the dénouement
And strategist
Signed up for the tempting abridged version
Which led him nowhere

At the end of the sullen mire
The spirometer's sphere entered peace.

## Pour Mamouque

Un papillon de paille habitait un crâne de chien
O couleurs ô jachère ô danse!

J'aime quand tu t'étonnes
Arcade sourcilière almée de l'amoureuse.

# For Mamouque

A butterfly made of straw lodged in a dog's skull
O colors o fallow land o dance!

I like to see you amazed
Eyebrow arch the lover's Egyptian dancing girl.

## CRÉSUS

### *à Georges Mounin*

Que la pourriture
Aux extrémités de radium
Aux clous mimétiques
Vous aspire
Poitrine en avance sur son néant
Espoir qu'une lame de limon inverse
Bouche d'air imagination

Enfants agile du boomerang
Longs amants aux plaisirs retirés
Filante vapeur insensible
Aux chairs agrandies pour la durée du sang
Aux successions hantées
A l'avenir fendu
Vous êtes le produit élevé de vos intègres défaillances
Virtuoses de l'élan visionnaires imprenables
Côte à côte dormez l'odyssée de l'amour
Les pièces de tourments éteintes
L'indiscernable blé de cratères
Croît en se consumant

Fossile frappé dans l'argile sentimentale
—Disons à toute épreuve l'étendue de l'amour—
Une femme suit des yeux l'homme vivant qu'elle aime
Baignée dans le sommeil qui lave les placers

## CROESUS

*for Georges Mounin*

Let decay
On radium grains
On mimetic nails
Suck you in
Chest ahead of its own void
The hope that a blade of silt inverts
Mouth of air, imagination

Boomerang's agile girls and boys
Long lovers with pleasures withdrawn
Gentle steam unmoved
By flesh engorged with the rush of blood
In haunted waves
In the fractured future
You are the costly result of your upright blackouts
Virtuosos of impulse, impregnable visionaries
Sleep side by side, the odyssey of love
Rooms of torture quenched
Imperceptible wheat of craters
Grows by burning up

Fossil struck in sentimental clay—
Let's say the rock solid extent of love—
A woman's eyes follow the living man whom she loves
Bathed in the sleep which cleans deposits of gold

À la faveur de l'abandon
Lui verse un léger malaise
Ha! comme il bombe la paupière
L'obstiné conventionnel

Assiette nue offerte à l'air
Au banc des mangeurs de poussière
Les mots restaurent l'Automate
Les mots à forte carrure s'empoignent sur le pont
    élastique
Qui mène au cloître du Cancer

Mains obscures mains si terribles
Filles d'excommuniés
Faites saigner les têtes chastes

Derrière les embruns on a nommé le sang
La chair toute puissante ranimée dans les rêves
Nourricière du phénix

Mort minuscule de l'été
Détèle-moi mort éclairante
A présent je sais vivre.

Making use of abandon
He's overcome by a light dizzy spell
Oh, how his eyelids flutter
Conventional, stubborn man

Bare plate offered up to the air
On the bench of those who eat dust
Words restore the Automaton
Words with muscular backs clash on the springy
    bridge
Which leads to the cloister of Cancer

Murky hands, dreadful hands
Daughters of men expelled from the church
Make chaste heads bleed

Behind the sea spray the blood was named
Almighty flesh revived in dreams
Sustaining the phoenix

Summer's minuscule death
Unhitch me, luminous death
Now I know how to live.

## Bourreaux de solitude

Le pas s'est éloigné le marcheur s'est tu
Sur le cadran de l'Imitation
Le Balancier lance sa charge de granit réflexe.

## Hangmen of Solitude

The footstep has drawn away, the walker grown still
On Imitation's face
The Pendulum throws its instinctive granite load.

## Versant

Donnons les prodiges à l'oubli secourable
Impavide
Laissons filer au blutoir des poussières les corps
    dont nous fûmes épris
Quittons ces fronts de chance plus souillés que les
    eaux
Noblesse de feuillage
À présent que décroît la portée de l'exemple
Quel carreau apparu en larmes
Va nous river
Coeurs partisans?

## Slope

Let's hand over marvels to helpful oblivion
Fearless
Let bodies we've loved
   spin on the sifter of dust
Let's retreat from these fronts of luck more soiled
   than streams
Grandeur of foliage
Now that the range of example declines
Which pane of glass appearing in tears
Will clinch us
Partisan hearts?

# Abondance Viendra

*à Paul Éluard*

# Abundance Will Come

*for Paul Éluard*

## L'Éclaircie

La vase sur la peau des reins, le gravier sur le nerf optique, tolérance et contenance. Absolue aridité, tu as absorbé toute la mémoire individuelle en la traversant. Tu t'es établie dans le voisinage des fontaines, autour de la conque, ce guêpier. Tu rumines. Tu t'orientes. Souveraine et mère d'un grand muet, l'homme te voit dans son rasoir, la compensation de sa disgrâce, d'une dynastie essentielle.

L'invincible dormeur enseignait que là où le mica était perméable aux larmes la présence de la mer ne s'expliquait pas. De nos jours, les mêmes oisifs, distinguent dans les fraîches cervelles innocentes les troubles insurmontables de l'âge futur. Symptômes de l'angoisse à l'extérieur des sépultures de l'ingénuité en extase;—ô profanation de l'esprit thermidor de famille, aurons-nous le temps de vous imposer notre grandeur?—L'intacte chrysalide a recouvré ses propriétés agissantes de vertige. La perforation des cellules du rayon, la traversée de la cheminée anathématisée, la reconnaissance des créances oubliées se poursuivent à travers les éclairs, le grésillement et la révélation de l'espèce fulgurante de grain solaire. Le sort de l'imagination adhérant sans réserves au développement d'un monde en tout renouvelé de l'attractif pourra être déterminé en cours de fouilles dans les archipels de l'estomac, à la suite de la brutale montée, à l'intelligence non soumise, du trésor sismique des famines.

## THE SUNNY SPELL

Mud on the skin of kidneys, grit on the optic nerve, forbearance and countenance. Total aridity, you have absorbed all personal memory while crossing through it. You have chosen to live close to underground springs, around the conch, this wasp nest. You brood. You get your bearings. You are mother and queen to a great man deprived of speech, who sees you in his razor blade, compensation for his shame, an essential dynasty.

The invincible sleeper taught that here, where mica permitted tears to pass through, the sea's presence was not explained. These days, the same idlers perceive in fresh innocent brains insurmountable hard times of a future age. Telltale signs of dread outside the graves of enraptured naiveté—o desecration of Thermidor spirit of family, will we have time to impose our grandeur upon you?—The pupa, intact, has recovered its active vertigo traits. Perforation of cells of the sun's ray, passage through vilified hearths, recognition of overdue debts continue through lightning flashes, the crackle and proof of the dazzling species of solar grain. Imagination's fate fully embracing the birth of a world of appeal, completely renewed, will be revealed when they excavate stomach archipelagos, after the brutal climb, with an untamed mind, of the seismic treasure of famines.

# Eaux-Mères

*À quoi je me destine*

La propriété de ma famille à l'Isle-sur-Sorgue. A l'ouest une vaste étendue de prairies. Le fourrage a été enlevé. Pour bien marquer les divisions, outre les rideaux d'arbres dépouillés de leurs feuilles, quelques sombres carrés de betteraves d'une espèce bâtarde, très basse. Tout cela rapidement aperçu. Je constate avec satisfaction que la vue est libre. À l'horizon et comme point final du panorama, une chaîne de montagnes me fait facilement songer à un renard bleu. Mon attention est attirée par un large fleuve sans sinuosité, qui s'avance vers moi, creusant son lit sur son passage. Son allure lente, mélancolique, est celle d'un promeneur un peu las. Je n'éprouve pas d'inquiétude. Quelques centaines de mètres me séparent de lui. En son milieu, marchant dans le sens du courant, de l'eau à la ceinture, je distingue, côte à côte, ma mère et mon neveu, ce dernier âgé de sept ans. Je remarque que le niveau de l'eau est le même pour tous les deux, bien qu'ils soient l'un et l'autre de taille visiblement différente. Ils me racontent la promenade qu'ils viennent de faire, promenade complètement dénuée d'intérêt, à mon avis. J'écoute très distraitement un récit où il est question d'un enfant que je ne connais pas, du nom de Louis Paul, disparu depuis peu de jours et dont on n'a pu réussir, malgré les efforts répétés et l'assurance qu'il s'est noyé dans le fleuve, à retrouver le corps. Ma mère se montre réservée dans le choix de ses termes. Systématiquement le mot «mort» n'est pas prononcé. Elle dit: «La perte du fil.» Ce qui me laisse rêveur. Je m'adresse à mon neveu: «Tâche, mon enfant, de ne pas égarer en crue la couleur de ta cravate».

# The Mother Liquor

*To what I intend to be*

My family's estate at Isle-sur-Sorgue. To the west, a vast expanse of pastures. The hay has been removed. To mark the divisions, in addition to the curtains of trees stripped of leaves, some dark squares of beets of a hybrid species, very low to the ground. All of this quickly taken in. With pleasure I note that the view is clear. On the horizon, and like a punctuation mark at the end of the vista, a chain of mountains makes me think of a blue fox. My attention is drawn to a broad river with no twists or turns coming toward me, digging its bed along the way. Its slow pace, melancholic, is that of a slightly weary hiker. I'm not alarmed. A few hundred meters still left between us. I make out the forms of my mother and nephew (seven years old), walking side by side along with the flow, in its center, water up to the waist. The water's rise is the same for both, though they're plainly of different heights. They talk of the walk they've just taken, a very boring walk in my opinion. I barely listen to their account of a child I've never met named Louis Paul who died a few days ago, and whose body was never retrieved, despite repeated attempts and the certain knowledge that he drowned in the river. My mother restrains herself in her choice of words. The word "death" is never uttered. She speaks of "the loss of the thread." Which leaves me dreamy. I speak to my nephew: "Try, my child, not to lose the color of your tie in the flood."

Dans les sous-sols de la maison d'habitation. Je suis dans une pièce infiniment peu attirante, probablement une ancienne cuisine désaffectée. Un alambic est accroché à un clou de la plinthe. Une corde à linge fortement nouée à ses deux extrémités traverse la pièce dans le sens de la largeur. Un placard dont on a ôté les battants—une forge et un étang—laisse voir à peu de distance un foyer de coke de gaz allumé et une pancarte, de la destination de celles des hommes-sandwich, sur laquelle est écrit en caractère Braille «Électricien de Vénus ». *J'ai l'impression que, mettant à profit la confusion qui règne, les vers de la farine ont dévoré le sel à l'Équateur.* Entre ma mère. Elle porte sans effort un cercueil de taille ordinaire qu'elle dépose, sans un mot, à mes pieds. Sa force m'est un profond sujet d'étonnement. En vain je m'essaie à soulever le cercueil. Cet objet *creux destiné à être longuement fécondé* me surprend par sa forme invariable et son aspect extérieur d'une grande propreté. On l'a passé à l'encaustique. Je suis flatté. Je questionne ma mère. Sur le ton de la conversation elle m'apprend la présence du cadavre de Louis Paul, *le bâtard d'eau*, à l'intérieur. Mais aussitôt elle détourne les yeux, très gênée et murmure à court de souffle: «C'est la logique», phrase que j'interprète par «c'est la guerre», et qui provoque ma colère. *Nous ne sommes donc pas sortis des frontières du Premier Empire.* Je désire m'assurer du contenu exact du cercueil. Je dévisse les écrous. Le cercueil est rempli d'eau. L'eau est extrêmement claire et transparente. Contrairement à celle du fleuve c'est une eau potable, probablement filtrée. Je me penche assez intrigué: sous l'eau, à quelques centimètres, dans une attitude de souffrance indescriptible, je distingue le corps d'un enfant d'une huitaine d'années. La position des membres, par ce qu'elle représente de désarticulation horrible, m'émeut vivement. Les chairs sont

In the cellars of the main house. I'm in a room that completely lacks appeal, most likely a kitchen that's old and condemned. Distilling equipment is hooked to the baseboard's nail. A clothes line tightly knotted at both ends crosses the breadth of the room. A cupboard whose doors have been removed—a forge and a pond—exposes nearby a lit charcoal hearth and a poster destined for men bearing sandwich-board signs, with Braille dots that spell "Electrician of Venus." *I have the hunch that, making the most of the reigning chaos, the flour worms have devoured the equator's salt.* My mother walks in. With no effort, she carries a casket of standard size which she sets down at my feet without a word. Her strength truly amazes me. I try in vain to lift the coffin. *This hollow object meant to be fertilized for ages* surprises me by its never-changing shape and its clean outward appearance. It's been waxed. I find it delightful. I question my mother. She casually lets me know that the corpse of Louis Paul, *water's bastard child,* is inside. But she instantly looks away, very embarrassed, and whispers, short of breath: "This is logic," a sentence I interpret as "this is war," which inflames my rage. *So we haven't broken free of the First Empire's bounds.* I want to be sure of the coffin's true contents. I unscrew the nuts. The coffin is filled with water. Extremely transparent water, and clear. Unlike the river, it's drinkable water, probably filtered. I bend down, quite intrigued: beneath the water, a few centimeters deep, in incredible suffering, a child's body, maybe eight years old. The horribly grim dislocation of arms and legs deeply moves me. The flesh is blue and black, torn, *since a struggle took place,* but strangely set, especially over the brow, taking on the design of Venetian lace. One of his arms is behind his head. His other hand is placed over his mouth, palm side up. His palm is a monkey's

bleues et noires, déchirées, *parce qu'il y a eu lutte*, mais curieusement disposées, en particulier sur le front où elles empruntent le dessin d'une dentelle vénitienne. L'un des bras passe derrière la tête. La main appliquée sur la bouche est retournée. La paume est un cul de singe. C'est le premier noyé qu'il m'est donné de voir: un monstre. Un chapeau de paille du genre canotier de premier communiant me surprend par son parfait état de conservation. Sur le ruban de couleur blanche, un mince filet de sang flotte sans parvenir à se détacher ni à troubler l'eau. C'est la sangsue *métisse*. Ma mère me prie de sortir. Je refuse. Elle attire mon attention sur ce qu'elle appelle tristement «Le retour des Boers (des bourgs?) fratricides». Elle tranche la corde *qui s'effondre avec un grand cri*. C'est un attentat. Quel poids! J'ai très peur. Je tire hâtivement le corps hors du cercueil. Durant cette opération, je pense, non sans mélancolie, à certaine mort vraiment trop inhumaine. L'essentiel est de ne pas échouer. Je comprends mal. Maintenant je frictionne rudement le corps de l'enfant. J'exécute à plusieurs reprises les tractions prévues de la langue. Mais je suis manifestement gêné, dominé par un sentiment de pudeur indicible. Ma mère se plaint de coliques. La raideur du corps de l'enfant s'est accrue. J'ai brusquement la conviction que cet enfant vit. *C'est l'évidence*. Tout à l'heure au fond de l'eau il louchait. *C'était l'octroi*. Je multiplie de plus en plus énergiquement mes frictions. Mais il faudrait qu'il rendît au moins une partie de l'eau absorbée. Sans cela il va couler de nouveau à pic. Sa bouche m'apparaît légèrement entr'ouverte. Où ai-je déjà vu ces lèvres? À Paris, au parc des Buttes-Chaumont, c'était l'arc du tunnel. Je guettais à l'entrée, la sourde et la muette, Je me rappelle avoir rêvé d'une exquise petite fille, *haute comme une bille*, se baignant dans la conque d'une source, toute nue. Malgré des séjours pro-

ass. It's the first drowning victim I've ever seen: a monster. A straw hat—the same boater kind worn by a child at first communion—surprises me by its perfectly preserved state. A thin trickle of blood floats on the white ribbon, but can't seem to get loose or disturb the water—the hybrid leech. My mother begs me to leave. I refuse. She draws my attention to what she ruefully calls "The return of fratricidal Boers (the burgs?)." She cuts the cord *which falls to the ground with a loud cry*. It's attempted murder. How heavy it is! I'm scared to death. I hastily pull the body out of the coffin. During this process, not without sadness, I think of a certain kind of death that's truly too inhumane. The key is not to fail. I don't really get it. I roughly rub the child's chest and limbs. I repeatedly pull on his tongue. But I'm clearly embarrassed, consumed by a sense of unspeakable modesty. My mother complains of gripping stomach pains. The child's stiffness has grown. All of a sudden I'm convinced this child's alive. *It's an obvious fact*. Earlier, down in the water, he squinted. *An excise tax*. With increasing force, I continue the rubdown. But he should have vomited some of the water absorbed. Or else he'll sink straight to the bottom once more. His mouth appears slightly open. Where have I seen those lips? In Paris, the Buttes-Chaumont Park—the tunnel's arch. I watched at the gate, the deaf and the mute. I recall a dream of a lovely young girl, *tall as a marble*, swimming nude in the conch of a spring. Despite long periods of time in the water, broken by frequent dives, she never managed to wet the outer lips of her sex, much to her distress. It was Sangŭe. What an adventure! *All around me it's raining soot and talc. Signs of alignment of stars in the sky, both auspicious and not so—unless day and night, sick of the present creation's conformity, haven't concluded the great pact of plenty.* This child's

longés dans l'eau, coupés de fréquents plongeons, elle n'était jamais parvenue qu'à mouiller les lèvres extérieures de son sexe et cela à son grand désespoir. C'était Sangüe. Quelle aventure! *Autour de moi il pleut de la suie et du talc. Signes d'une conjonction d'astres dans le ciel favorable et défavorable; à moins que le jour et la nuit écœurés du conformisme de l'actuelle création n'aient enfin conclu le grand pacte d'abondance.* Il n'y a rien de miraculeux dans le retour à la vie de cet enfant. Je méprise les esprits religieux et leurs interprétations mystiques. Je prends l'enfant dans mes bras et une immense douceur m'envahit. J'aime cet enfant d'un amour maternel, d'une grandeur impossible à concevoir. Il va falloir changer ma règle d'existence. Ma tâche est désormais de le protéger. Il est menacé. On verra. Il est petit et je suis grand. Assis sur une chaise et le serrant contre moi, je le berce tendrement. Ma sœur, mère de mon neveu, se trouve là. Je la prie de m'apporter des vêtements secs. Il me tarde qu'elle me donne satisfaction pour la mettre dehors ensuite. Elle ne se montre pas très empressée. À cette minute je mesure toute l'étendue de son avarice. Je la menace de la tuer. Elle s'en va et revient bientôt avec un gracieux vêtement taillé dans un fibrôme *d'été.* Elle fait preuve dans ses explications d'une platitude et d'une bassesse odieuses. Il semble que l'enfant sur mes genoux s'est transformé. Son visage vivant, expressif, ses cheveux châtains, en particulier, m'enchantent. Ils sont partagés par une raie impeccable. L'enfant m'aime profondément. Il me dit sa confiance et se blottit contre moi. Je suis ému aux larmes. Nous ne nous embrassons pas. Ma mère et ma sœur ont disparu. A la place qu'elles occupaient il y a une loupe noire, monnaie d'arcane oubliée *par le libérateur repoussant.*

return to life is not a miracle. I despise religious minds and their mystical takes. I gather the child into my arms and overwhelming gentleness fills me. The maternal love I have for this child is beyond measure. I'll have to change the course of my life. My task from now on is to keep him safe. He's at risk. Wait and see. He's small and I'm big. Hunched on a chair and clutching him against my chest, I lull him with love. My sister, my nephew's mother, is here. I beg her to fetch some dry clothes. I'm anxious for her to comply so I can quickly get rid of her. She doesn't seem eager to do what I've asked. In this moment I realize the full extent of her greed. I threaten to kill her. She runs off and soon returns with a graceful garment cut from a fibrous tumor *of summer*. Her explanations are trite and hatefully mean. It seems that the child on my lap has changed. I am filled with joy by his face full of life—so expressive—especially his chestnut brown hair with a perfect part. The child loves me deeply. He shows me his trust and cuddles against me. I am moved to tears. We don't kiss. My mother and sister are gone. Where they stood is a flawed black precious stone, *the repulsive liberator's* cryptic currency left behind.

## LES RAPPORTS ENTRE PARASITES

Historien aux abois, frère, fuyard, étrangle ton maître. Sa cuirasse n'est qu'une croûte. Il a pourri la santé publique. Autrement tu sombrais dans la tendresse. Entre les cuisses du crucifié se balance ta tête créole de poète. La lave adorable dissout la roche florissante.

L'ennemi barbouillé de rouille est coiffé d'une peau de porc-épic. Il est naturel depuis le naufrage de la justice. Il se passionne pour les infirmes. C'est une loque. Il vole les boueux. C'est une crapule. Il aime se clapir dans les plis des torchons. C'est un solitaire. Ce dieu n'a jamais osé respirer un mort intentionnel. C'est un lâche.

Le cadavre récréatif, une fois encore, va passer dans toutes les mains. C'est la ruine des orphelins. Il faut être un fœtus pour croire à l'action corrosive des buées. Que la cagoule se détraque.

· · · · · · · · · · · · · · · · · · · · · · · · · · · · · · · · · · · · · · · · · · · · · · · · · · ·

Témoin, dans les relais de ton esprit réaliste, le règne végétal est figuré par la plante carnivore, le règne minéral par le radium sauvage, le règne animal par l'ascendant du tigre. Bâtir une postérité sans amertume. Témoin antédiluvien tu flattes ma maladresse. Gagne, je te prie, tes tuiles transparentes. De là, tu vas pouvoir suivre paisiblement les évolutions mortelles du réfractaire.

Ce matin, le citronnier des murailles donnait des fruits buboniques. Derrière les arbres civilisés, une équipe d'ouvriers équarrissait la boue, cette autre pierre précieuse. L'homme restitue l'eau comme le ciel. Pour être logique avec la nature, il sème des lueurs et récolte des épieux. Seule le désempare quelquefois, au seuil de l'envoûtement, l'absence de ressemblance. Ainsi ce

## Relations Between Parasites

Despairing historian, brother, deserter, strangle your master. His armor is just a crust. It has rotted public health. Otherwise, you sank into tenderness. Your creole head of a poet swings between thighs of the crucified. Lovable lava dissolves the thriving rock.

The enemy smeared with rust is wearing a porcupine hide. It's natural since the collapse of justice. He's fervent about the infirm. He's a wreck. He steals those covered with mud. He's a low life. He likes to conceal himself in the folds of dishrags. He's a loner. This god has never dared to inhale an intentional death. He's a coward.

The amusing corpse will pass through all hands once more. He's the ruin of orphans. You must be a fetus to trust in the caustic action of steam. Let the cowl come undone.

. . . . . . . . . . . . . . . . . . . . . . . . . . . . . . . . . . . . . . . . . . . . . . . . . . . .

Witness, in your realist mind's relays, the vegetable kingdom is portrayed by carnivorous plants, the mineral kingdom by wild radium, the animal kingdom by tigers' forebears. To build a posterity free of rancor. Antediluvian witness, you flatter my awkwardness. Please overcome your transparent bad luck. From there, you'll be able to quietly watch the mortal evolutions of those who resist.

This morning, the high wall's lemon trees bore bubonic fruits. Behind the civilized trees, a team of workers squared off the mud, that other precious stone. Man restores the water like the sky. To apply reason to nature, he sows flashes of light and harvests spears. He's only confused sometimes, on the brink of a spell, by the absence of likeness. So this tale limps away. The hand of justice has tried to keep the arsonist lens, color of air, at an equal

conte s'éloigne en boitant. La main de justice a bien essayé de maintenir à égale distance du Soleil et du Parlement la loupe incendiaire, couleur d'air. Bulles. Mais aucune indignité ne souille les correspondances. Cette nuit, au faîte de sa splendeur, mon amour aura à choisir entre deux grains également sordides de poussière. Les chaînes magnétiques naviguent loin des feux commandés. À la question, le désespoir ne se rétracte que pour avouer le désespoir.

distance from Sun and Parliament. Bubbles. But no shameful act taints the connections. Tonight, at the height of her glory, my love must choose between two equally sordid specks of dust. Magnetic chains sail far from controlled fires. When tortured, despair only recants to confess to despair.

## MIGRATION

*à Yvonne Zervos*

Le poids du raisin modifie la position des feuilles. La montagne avait un peu glissé. Sans dégager d'époque. Toutefois, à travers les ossuaires argileux, la foulée des bêtes excrémentielles en marche vers le convulsif ambre jaune. En relation avec l'inerte.

La sécurité est un parfum. L'homme morne et emblématique vit toujours en prison, mais sa prison se trouve à présent en liberté. Le mouvement et le sentiment ont réintégré la fronde mathématicienne. La fabuleuse simulatrice, celle qui s'ensevelit en marchant, qui remporta dans la nuit tragique de la préhistoire les quatre doigts tabous de la main-fantôme, a rejoint ses quartiers d'étude, à la zone des clairvoyances. Dans le salon manqué, sur les grands carreaux hostiles, le dormeur et l'aimée, trop impopulaires pour ne pas être réels, accouplent interminablement leurs bouches ruisselantes de salive.

## MIGRATION

*for Yvonne Zervos*

Weight of the grape transforms the position of leaves. The mountain had slightly slipped. Without dislodging an epoch. However, across clay-lined heaps of bones, excremental beasts' tread on the move toward convulsive yellow amber. Relating with the inert.

Security is a perfume. Bleak and symbolic man still lives in prison, but a prison at present found in freedom. Movement and feeling restored the Newtonian slingshot. The mythical faker who buried herself while walking, carrying back in prehistory's tragic night the four taboo fingers on the phantom hand, has returned to her study, within the clairvoyants' zone. In the failed living room, on the great hostile tiles, the one who sleeps and the one who is loved, both too unpopular not to be real, endlessly couple their mouths dripping wet with saliva.

## DOMAINE

Tombe mars fécond sur le toit de chagrin. La lampe retournée ne fume plus. Les nobles disparus ont curé les bassins, vidé les flasques horreurs domestiques, brossé l'obèse. Pomme de terre de semence est devenue folle.

Matériaux vacillants, portes, coulisses, soupiraux, réduits comme je voudrais pouvoir régler mon allure suivant la vôtre. Jamais de double voix, cet impair larmoyant. Je feindrais l'impéritie des signes. Survivant, je saurais m'alléger de l'allégresse déprimante, pistil de l'enfance. Je murerais mon blason sanglant. Jusqu'à la rumeur artificielle de cette peau de sagesse vaniteuse torréfiée sur les tisons comme une glaire.

Sur une vanne aérienne, passerelle verticale, cette combinaison de lettres bouillantes: DÉPÔT D'EXCLUS. Passives mémoires de bois blanc pour le rachat des morgues et l'entretien des patries. Granit, arc-en-ciel, tu auras lacé leurs fantasmes pédestres jusqu'au sable . . .

Une allumette bien prise a débouclé le carcan, biceps et coude. Le leader a tiré la vermine éclairante. C'est la lave finale. Régicide, estime-toi favorisé si une langue de bœuf vient de loin en loin égayer ta cuvette.

Ma maîtresse mouillée, écorchée insultante, je te plante dans mon cri. Ainsi tu tiens à moi fumée affectueuse, indice d'immémoriale, d'ondoyante blancheur, lorsque la première source s'élançait, flotteur d'alarme, sur une pente disparue. Je me

# DOMAIN

March falls fruitful on sorrow's roof. The inverted lamp no longer smokes. Lords and ladies gone missing have scraped the basins clean, have drained the flasks—domestic eyesores—and scrubbed the obese. Seed potato has grown mad.

Unsteady materials, doors, backstage wings, basement windows, corners, how I wish I could set my pace to yours. Never with double voice, that tearful faux pas. I'd fake a lack of talent for signs. Survivor, I'd free myself from depressing glee, pistil of childhood. I'd wall in my coat of arms, covered with blood. Until the contrived distant sound of that skin of vain wisdom, grilled like the white of an egg on a dying flame.

On an aerial valve, vertical footbridge, this arrangement of passionate letters: DEPOT FOR OUTCASTS. Passive memories of white wood for ransom of morgues and the upkeep of native lands. Granite, rainbow, you will have tied their pedestrian fantasies up to the sand . . .

A well-lit match has undone biceps, elbow and iron restraints. The leader has drawn forth the enlightening vermin. It's the final lava. Regicide, think yourself held in high esteem if a beef tongue comes from far away to brighten your bowl.

My moistened mistress, insulting thin-skinned one, I plant you in my cry. In this way, I am dear to you, loving smoke, clue of timelessness, shimmering whiteness, when the first spring rushed forth, warning float, toward a vanished slope. I turn to-

tourne vers toi, Sainte de manufacture, grise mine au sein sec, diseuse de solfège. Tu ronfles, matraque, pour le miracle de l'hélice . . . Quelle mélopée!

Mes songes, hors amour, étaient graves et distants.

Faut-il *malgré* se réjouir?

ward you, Saint of production, who pulls a long face with a hard heart, the one who recites solfège. You whir, blunt club, for wondrous propellers . . . What a monotonous chant!

My dreams, outside of love, were grave and remote.

Should we *despite* be glad?

## INTÉGRATION

*à Christian Zervos*

Le souffle abdique sur la cendre. Au point de panique, l'exploitation des fléaux progresse à la vitesse du microscope. Dans l'œil immuablement clos, ce premier jour d'hiver, le livre d'or est un kaki.

Grand tronc en activité crois-tu au dénouement par la lèpre?

Banquises indissolubles, dans vos mers clôturées se résorbe la honte. Songes tirés des perversions immortelles, juste cible au bas du ventre qui déferle, les artères crèvent les Tours de Copernic. Forteresse défroquée. La braise lilliputienne fusionne avec le sang. Pénultième vérité, qui vas-tu instruire? Amalgame ignoré, veux-tu m'accueillir?

Craie, qui parla sur les tableaux noirs une langue plastique dérivée du naphte—auditoire civil, de santé moyenne—j'évoque les charmes de tes épaisseurs voilées, siège de la cabale. Nous fûmes le théâtre d'étranges secousses : poitrine livide nettoyée de son amour, déchéance simulée pour défendre l'accès au gisement. Le scarabée fuyant le lierre, en vue de tes contreforts embrasés, se retourne sur le dos, moteur ébloui, et raccorde. Midi réhabilité.

Craie, enrôle-moi, cadavre, dans ton principe, afin que l'armée victorieuse des insurgés ne bute pas contre les degrés de mon armature.

## INTEGRATIVE

*for Christian Zervos*

Breath surrenders on ash. To the point of panic, the growing of plagues evolves at microscopic speed. In the steadfast closed eye, on that first winter's day, the guestbook is a kaki.

Great trunk in activity, do you believe in the ending by leprosy?

Indissoluble ice floes, shame is resorbed in your closed seas. Dreams drawn from undying perversions, perfect target unfurls on the lower belly, arteries burst the Copernicus Towers. Defrocked fortress. The Lilliputian embers fuse with blood. Penultimate truth, who will you teach? Unknown amalgam, do you want to greet me?

Chalk, which spoke on blackboards a malleable language derived from naphtha—civilian audience, of average health—I conjure up spells of your veiled thicknesses, siege of cabals. We were the theater of strange shocks: deathly pale chest cleaned from its love, decadence feigned to protect access to mineral veins. The Japanese beetle fleeing the ivy, seeing your foothills set ablaze, turns on its back, dazzled engine, and connects. Noon restored.

Chalk, enlist me, corpse, to your cause, so the victorious rebel army won't stumble over my armature's layered defense.

## Devant soi

Les battues à travers les fabriques véreuses, à la recherche de moutures, chimères désarmées, signes errants d'intelligence naufragés au bord des yeux, phalanges imperceptibles. Sources, dans la perméabilité de vos sables, un clair désespoir a enfoui ses œufs.

La rage a creusé ton ventre nubile, chloroformé ton cœur, dénaturé tes songes. La crampe a éduqué tes mains contradictoires. De la sorte furent dragués les calculs dans les bauges, chatouillés les pourrissoirs aux aveuglantes déflagrations. O sordide indicible! Sommeil d'aliéné commué en réalité ouvrière . . . Ensuite, de vagues grandes femmes blanches, tirées par des vœux, s'élancèrent des créneaux, fendirent la mer—la mer fixe des templiers!—saluèrent.

Une société bien vêtue a horreur de la flamme. La corbeille de tes noces, extraite du columbarium, fut versée à la fosse commune. L'amertume pacifiée . . .

Équarrisseur, ta descendance s'est éteinte. Malgré tes contractions, la lente retraite chiffonnière s'écoule acclamant au passage le déclin de l'Élagueur. Le catafalque habituel est dressé sous la voûte de bienfaisance.

Amour réduit à ma merci, que dirais-tu d'un château ultra-violet en amont d'un bourg dévasté par le typhus? Cela se visite.

## AHEAD OF YOU

Searches through worm-eaten mills, seeking subsequent drafts, disarmed fantasies, stray signs of intelligence shipwrecked at the edge of eyes, phalanges that can't be seen. Underground springs—in your permeable sands, a pale despair has buried its eggs.

Rage has hollowed out your nubile belly, chloroformed your heart, distorted your dreams. Cramps have informed your contradictory hands. In this way, concretions were dredged in wallows, and heaps of decay were tickled with blinding explosions. O sordid unspeakable! Sleep of a madman commuted to laborer life . . . Large indistinct white women, tugged by vows, rushed forward from crenels, cleaved the sea—the resolute sea of the Templars!—waved.

A well-dressed society hates the flame. Your wedding presents, removed from the niche of the burial vault, were poured into the mass grave. Rancor appeased.

Knacker, your family line is extinct. Despite your diminished state, the slow retreat of the ragman flows by, cheering the Tree Trimmer's decline. Erected under charity's arch, the usual catafalque.

Love left to my mercy, what would you say of an ultraviolet castle upstream from a town ravaged by typhus? Something that must be seen.

# Notes

"Masque de fer" / "Iron Mask"
Translator's note: This poem refers to the legend of the "Man in the Iron Mask," about a political prisoner whose identity was kept secret in France during the reign of Louis XIV.

"Artine" / "Artine"
Translator's note: *Nature-précise* plays on the phrase *nature morte* (still-life).

"Poème" / "Poem"
Poet's note, from the original publication, quote attributed to Albert-Le-Grand: "*Il y avait en Allemagne deux enfants jumeaux, dont l'un ouvrait les portes en les touchant avec son bras droit, l'autre les fermait en les touchant avec son bras gauche.*" ("There were two twin children in Germany; one would open doors by touching them with his right arm, while the other would close them using his left arm.")

"La Main de Lacenaire" / "Lacenaire's Hand"
Translator's note: Pierre François Lacenaire (1805–1836) was a French poet and notorious social rebel whose hand was severed after his execution for murder.

"Les Observateurs et les rêveurs" / "Observers and Dreamers"
Translator's note: Maurice Blanchard was a French visual artist.

"Confronts" / "Confrontations"
Translator's note: Marcel Fourrier was one of the writers who
signed the second manifesto of Surrealism.

"Sade, l'amour enfin sauvé de la boue du ciel, cet héritage suffira
aux hommes contre la famine" / "Sade, Love Finally Saved from
the Mud of the Sky, This Legacy Will Suffice for Men Against
Hunger"
Translator's note: Maurice Heine was a French editor and
writer.

"Pour Mamouque" / "For Mamouque"
Translator's note: "Mamouque" was the nickname of Char's
first wife, Georgette Goldstein, whom he married in 1932.

"Crésus" / "Croesus"
Translator's Note: Croesus, king of Lydia from 560 BC to 547
BC, was known for his great wealth. Misinterpreting the Oracle
at Delphi, he was defeated by the Persians.
Georges Mounin (1910–1993) was a French professor of
linguistics who greatly admired Char's work.

"Eaux-mères" / "The Mother Liquor"
Poet's note, from the original publication: *Ce texte dans son
ensemble est un récit de rêve. Seules les parties en italiques sont
des impressions de réveil qui se sont imposées à mon esprit au fur
et à mesure de la transcription du rêve. Je n'ai pas cru devoir les
écarter tant elles mettaient d'insistance à être consignées. On les
trouvera scrupuleusement dans l'ordre.* (This text, as a whole, is
a dream narrative. Only the parts in italics are the impressions

that came to me upon awakening, as I wrote down the dream.
I felt I should not dismiss them, as they emphatically asked to
be recorded. They are herein transcribed in the strict order in
which they came.)

"Migration" / "Migration"
Translator's note: Yvonne Zervos, one of Char's close friends,
befriended many poets and painters of her time.

"Intégration" / "Integrative"
Translator's note: Christian Zervos was the founder and (with
Yvonne Zervos) co-publisher of the magazine *Cahiers d'art*, to
which Char contributed.

## Acknowledgments

Grateful acknowledgment is made to the editors of the following journals in which these translations previously appeared.

*American Poetry Review*: "Confrontations," "Cooled Metals," "Croesus," "Jagged," "Pruner's Daeresis," "Singular," "Slope," and "Stern Lesson"

*Bat City Review*: "Migration" and "On the Remarkable Horizon"

*Circumference*: "The Dismissed Instructor"

*Crazyhorse*: "Chain"

*cream city review*: "Hangmen of Solitude" and "The Prodigal's Torch"

*Eleven Eleven*: "The Sunny Spell"

*Field*: "Artine"

*Five Points*: "Continuous Truth," "Fatal Sleep," and "Possible"

*Ilanot Review*: "Observers and Dreamers"

*The Iowa Review*: "Lust" and "The Violent Rose"

*The Journal*: "Double" and "Robust Meteors"

*Kenyon Review Online*: "Sade, Love Finally Saved from the Mud, this Legacy Will Suffice for Men Against Hunger"

*Lake Effect*: "Ahead of You"

*The Laurel Review*: "The Climate of Hunting or How Poems Are Made," "The Historian" (as "The Female Historian"), "The Manna of Lola Abba," and "Poem"

*Loch Raven Review*: "Alive Tomorrow," "Chain," "The Dismissed Instructor," and "You Open Your Eyes"

*Massachusetts Review*: "The Mother Liquor"

*Mead*: "Barbaric Leaven," "Frenetic Poetry's Messengers" and "Iron Mask"

*Mid-American Review*: "Men Without Shadows (Equator Dwellers)" and "Summary"

*Notre Dame Review*: "Oracle of the Great Orange Tree" and "Poets"

*Sakura Review*: "Melodious Suns" and "Premonitions and Stately Building"

*The Southeast Review*: "Cruelty," "Improvised Torture," and "Relations between Parasites"

*Sycamore Review*: "Here"

*Taos Journal of International Poetry & Art*: "Domain," "The Enraged Craftsmanship," "For Mamouque," and "Integrative"

*Witness*: "Alive Tomorrow"

In addition, "Alive Tomorrow," "Chain," "The Dismissed Instructor," "Here," and "You Open Your Eyes" appeared in *Stone Lyre: Poems of René Char* (Tupelo Press, 2010).

These translations are dedicated with love to the memory of my father, Robert Lipton (1921–2014), and my cousin, Alex Federman (1991–2015).

I am deeply grateful to my husband, Ted Miller, whose love enables me to pursue my writing life, as he is always there when I come up for air. Many thanks to my children Rachel and Seth for their support, as well as to my mother, a past president of the American Association of Teachers of French (AATF), who encouraged me to learn French.

I thank editors Sven Birkerts, Jim Hicks, and G. C. Waldrep for their support and unflagging love for the writings of René Char, and I am grateful to Ivan de Monbrison for his help with these difficult French texts. Thanks also to Catherine Maigret Kellogg for her proofing that left no accent mark misplaced.

Finally, as ever, my unending gratitude to Tupelo Press for making such beautifully crafted books, and to Jeffrey Levine for his literary genius and acumen, as well as to Jim Schley, masterful editor and *fervent de Char*; to Josef Beery, brilliant designer of the cover and text; and to Marie Gauthier for her ability to magically make things happen.

## OTHER BOOKS FROM TUPELO PRESS

*Another English: Anglophone Poems from Around the World* (anthology), edited by Catherine Barnett and Tiphanie Yanique

*Personal Science* (poems), Lillian-Yvonne Bertram

*Everything Broken Up Dances* (poems), James Byrne

*One Hundred Hungers* (poems), Lauren Camp

*My Immaculate Assassin* (novel), David Huddle

*Dancing in Odessa* (poems), Ilya Kaminsky

*A God in the House: Poets Talk About Faith* (interviews), edited by Ilya Kaminsky and Katherine Towler

*Third Voice* (poems), Ruth Ellen Kocher

*Boat* (poems), Christopher Merrill

*Yes Thorn* (poems), Amy Munson

*Lucky Fish* (poems), Aimee Nezhukumatathil

*The Ladder* (poems), Alan Michael Parker

*Why Don't We Say What We Mean?* (essays), Lawrence Raab

*Intimate: An American Family Photo Album* (hybrid memoir), Paisley Rekdal

*Wintering* (poems), Megan Snyder-Camp

*Walking Backwards* (poems), Lee Sharkey

*Swallowing the Sea* (essays), Lee Upton


*See our complete list at www.tupelopress.org*

CPSIA information can be obtained
at www.ICGtesting.com
Printed in the USA
BVHW020052210122
625948BV00005B/18